# 1, 2, 3, GO!

## Huy Voun Lee

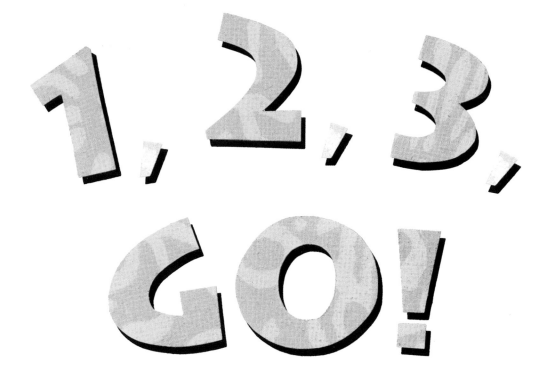

HENRY HOLT AND COMPANY   ◆   NEW YORK

## Author's Note

There are many different dialects spoken in China, but the written language is always the same. Each written word, or character, is based on a drawing of an object or an idea. Some of the basic characters, such as "child" 子 and "tree" 木, still bear a resemblance to what the object looks like or the idea it represents, while other characters have changed beyond recognition. The secret of learning new characters is knowing how to combine these basic characters. When you see characters that contain the basic character for tree, their meaning has something to do with wood. For example, the character for "plum" 李 is composed of the basic characters for child and tree, because Chinese children love plums, and plums grow on trees. Sometimes a basic character is present not because of its meaning, but because the sound of the word is similar to the sound of the basic character.

| | | |
|---|---|---|
| 手 | hand | shǒu (show) |
| 足 | foot | zú (tsoo) |
| 捉 | catch | zhuō (zhwo) |
| 踏 | stomp | dà (da) |
| 打 | hit | dǎ (da) |
| 推 | push | tuī (tway) |
| 提 | carry | tí (tee) |
| 拉 | pull | lā (la) |
| 蹑 | tiptoe | niè (nee'eh) |
| 跳 | jump | tiào (tee'ow) |
| 踢 | kick | tī (tee) |
| 跑 | run | pǎo (pow) |

Pronunciations in parentheses are approximations of Mandarin Chinese.

For Raymond,
who's full of happy hands and jumpy feet!
Love always, Auntie Huy

Henry Holt and Company, LLC
*Publishers since 1866*
175 Fifth Avenue, New York, New York 10010
www.henryholt.com

Henry Holt is a registered trademark of Henry Holt and Company, LLC
Copyright © 2000 by Huy Voun Lee. All rights reserved.
Distributed in Canada by H. B. Fenn and Company Ltd.

Library of Congress Cataloging-in-Publication Data
Lee, Huy Voun. 1, 2, 3, go! / Huy Voun Lee.
Summary: An introduction to Chinese writing describing
the construction, meaning, and pronunciation of simple characters
used for a variety of words and the numbers one through ten.
ISBN-13: 978-0-8050-6205-2 / ISBN-10: 0-8050-6205-X
1. Chinese characters—Juvenile literature. [1. Chinese characters.
2. Counting.] I. Title: One, two, three, go. II. Title.
PL1171.L328    2000    495.1'82421—dc21    99-48326
First Edition—2000 / Designed by Donna Mark
Manufactured in China
3   5   7   9   10   8   6   4

The artist used cut-paper collage to create
the illustrations for this book.

As you read this book, pay attention to the action characters. Words such as "kick," "run," and "jump" all have to do with feet, so the characters for these words include the basic character for "foot" 足. The characters for words such as "throw," "carry," and "push," which have to do with hands, all include the basic character for "hand" 手.

One catches.

一
one

捉
catch

# Two stomp.

二
two

踏
stomp

三
three

打
hit

Three hit.

# Four push.

四
four

推
push

Five carry.

五

five

carry

# Six pull.

六
six

拉
pull

*Seven tiptoe.*

七
seven

蹑
tiptoe

*Eight jump.*

八

跳

*Nine kick.*

九

nine

踢

kick

# Ten run.

十
ten

跑
run

*Go!*

去

go

| 一 | one | yī<br>(ee) |
| 二 | two | èr<br>(er) |
| 三 | three | sān<br>(san) |
| 四 | four | sì<br>(ss'uh) |
| 五 | five | wǔ<br>(woo) |
| 六 | six | liù<br>(liu) |
| 七 | seven | qī<br>(chi) |
| 八 | eight | bā<br>(ba) |
| 九 | nine | jiǔ<br>(jiu) |
| 十 | ten | shí<br>(ssh'uh) |
| 去 | go | qù<br>(ch'oo, *pronounced*<br>*with rounded lips*) |